# Math in Focus

## Singapore Math
### by Marshall Cavendish

## Extra Practice

**KB**

**Author**
Dr. Pamela Sharpe

 **Marshall Cavendish**
Education

**US Distributor**

HOUGHTON MIFFLIN HARCOURT

COMMON CORE

© 2012 Marshall Cavendish International (Singapore) Private Limited

**Published by Marshall Cavendish Education**
*An imprint of Marshall Cavendish International (Singapore) Private Limited*
Times Centre, 1 New Industrial Road, Singapore 536196
Customer Service Hotline: (65) 6411 0820
E-mail: tmesales@sg.marshallcavendish.com
Website: www.marshallcavendish.com/education

Distributed by
**Houghton Mifflin Harcourt**
222 Berkeley Street
Boston, MA 02116
Tel: 617-351-5000
Website: www.hmheducation.com/mathinfocus

Second edition 2012

Marshall Cavendish and *Math in Focus* are registered trademarks of Times Publishing Limited

*Math in Focus*® Kindergarten Extra Practice B
ISBN 978-0-547-67905-1

Printed in Singapore

4  5  6  7  8          1897      16  15  14  13  12
4500367000                       B  C  D  E

# Contents

## CHAPTER 15   Length and Height

## CHAPTER 16   Classifying and Sorting

## CHAPTER 17   Addition Stories

# Subtraction Stories

# Measurement

# Money

# Introducing

# Math in Focus®

## Extra Practice KB

*Extra Practice KB* is written to complement the *Math in Focus®: Singapore Math by Marshall Cavendish* Kindergarten program.

*Extra Practice KB* provides questions to reinforce the concepts taught, and can be used to assess children's understanding after each day.

*Extra Practice KB* is an excellent option for homework, or may be used in class or after school. It is intended for children who simply need more practice to become confident, or secure children who are aiming for excellence.

BLANK

# CHAPTER 7 Solid and Flat Shapes

## Lesson 1  Solid Shapes

## Match.

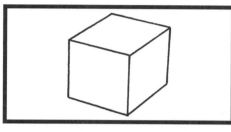 •     •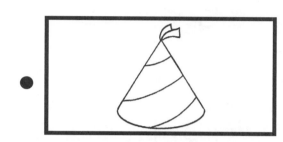

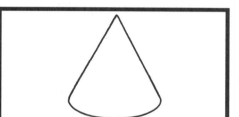 •     •

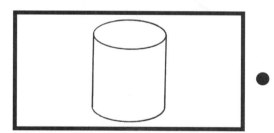 •     •

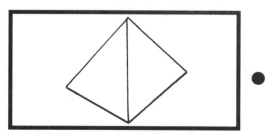 •     •

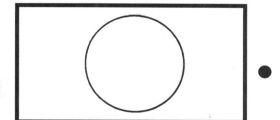 •     •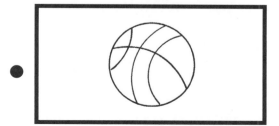

# How many are there? Count and write.

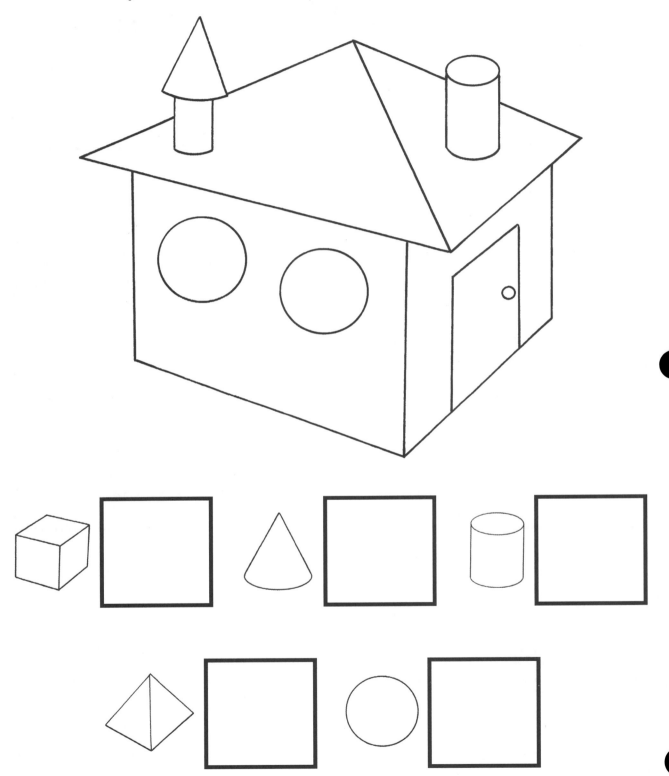

Name: _____

## Lesson 2 Flat Shapes in Solid Shapes

# Match.

# Match.

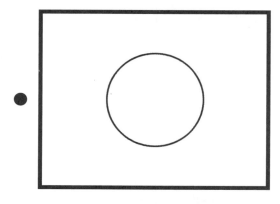

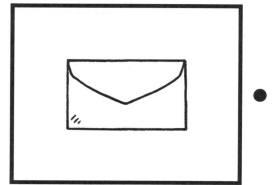

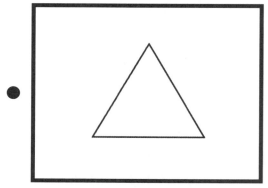

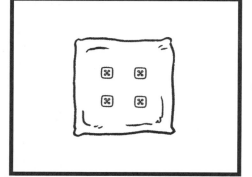

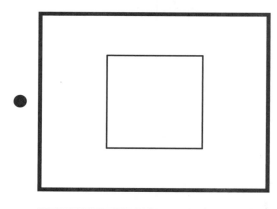

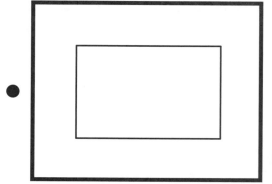

## Lesson 3  Flat Shapes

# Match.

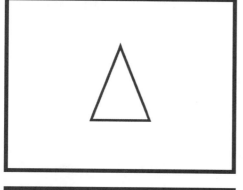

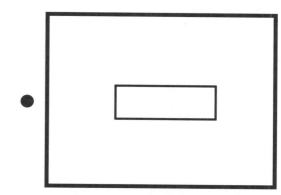

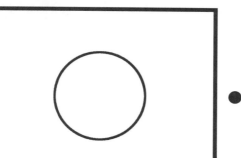

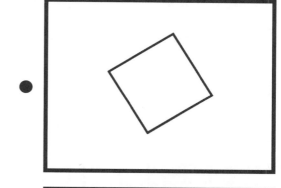

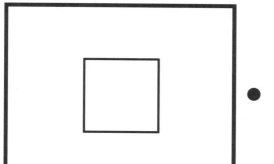

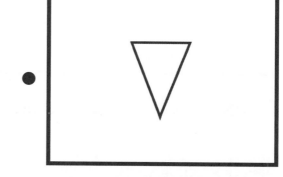

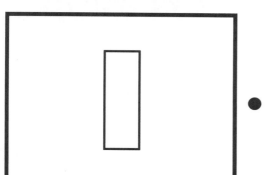

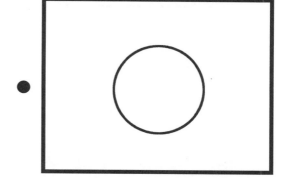

Name: _____

## Color the **big** circle.

## Color the **small** square.

## Color the **big** rectangle.

Name: _____

# Color the squares red. Color the rectangles green. Color the circles yellow. Color the triangles blue.

# How many are there? Count and write.

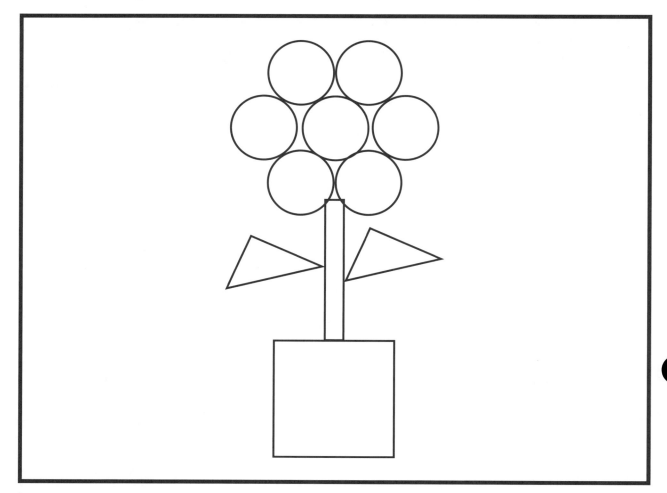

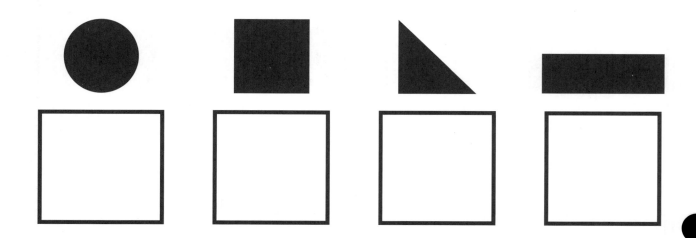

## Lesson 5 Shape Patterns

## Complete the patterns.

 **1**

 **2**

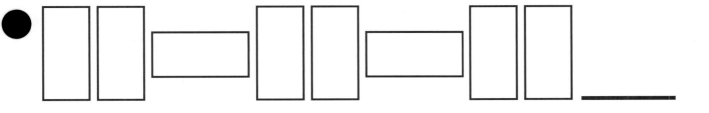

 **3**

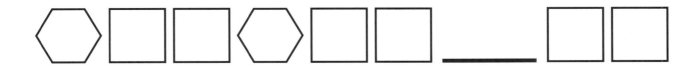

# Complete the patterns.

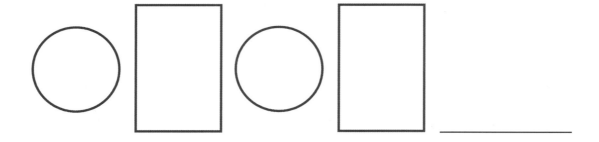

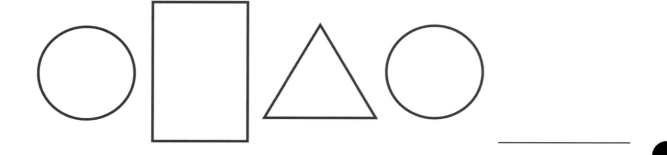

# CHAPTER 8 Numbers to 100

## Lesson 1 Counting by 2s

### Match. Count by 2s and write.

 •          •

 •          •

 •          •

 •          •

 •          •

## How many in all? _____

# Count and write.

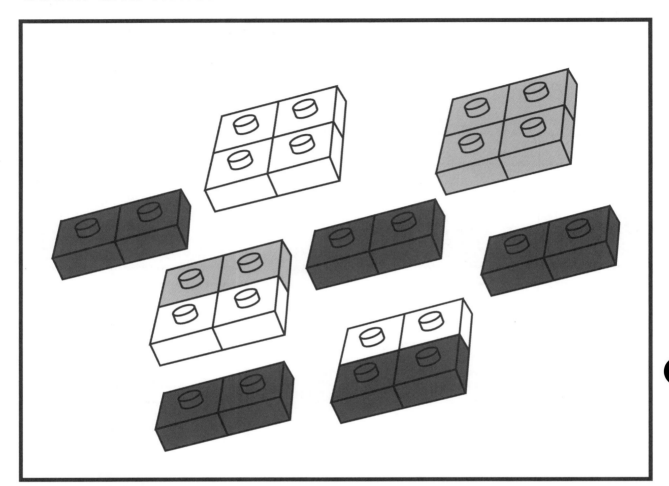

```
┌──────────┐    ┌──────────┐    ┌──────────┐
│          │    │          │    │          │
│          │    │          │    │          │
└──────────┘    └──────────┘    └──────────┘
```

## Lesson 2  Counting by 5s

# Count by 2s or count by 5s? Put a ✔.

 **1**

| 2s | |
|---|---|

| 5s | |
|---|---|

 **2**

| 2s | |
|---|---|

| 5s | |
|---|---|

 **3**

| 2s | |
|---|---|

| 5s | |
|---|---|

# Circle the groups of 5 apples.

# Make the tally.

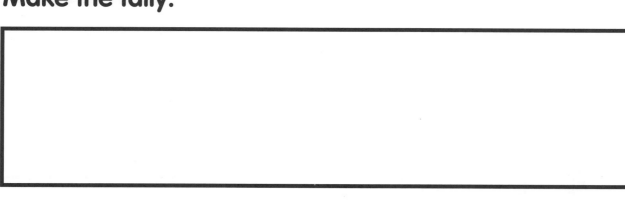

## Lesson 3  Counting by 10s to 100

# Circle 70.

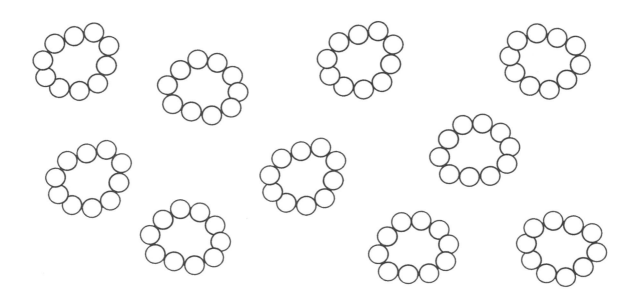

# Circle 50.

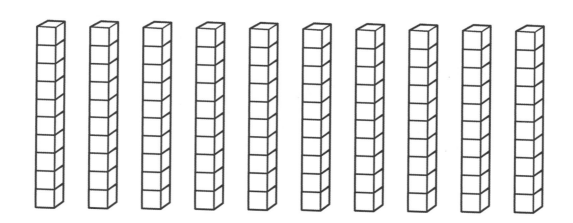

# Circle groups of 10. Then, count and circle.

How many in all?    15    22    25    28

## Lesson 4  Numbers 20 to 49

## Color.

 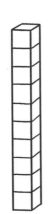   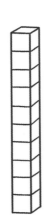

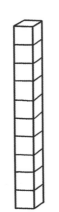 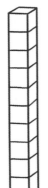 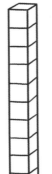  

# What comes next? Put a ✔.

 **1**

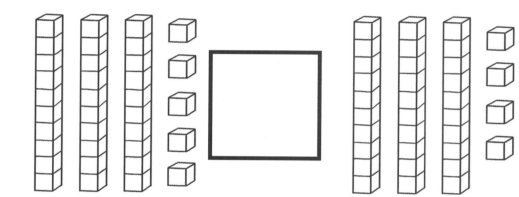

---

 **2**

29

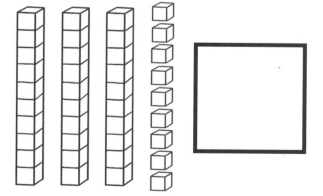

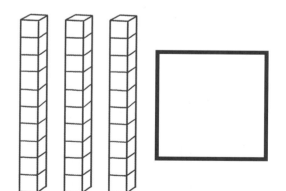

Name: _____

# Color the missing number.

**1** 22, 23,

| 24 |
|----|
| 34 |
| 42 |

, 25, 26

**2** 29,

| 20 |
|----|
| 38 |
| 30 |

, 31, 32, 33

**3** 45, 46, 47, 48,

| 44 |
|----|
| 49 |
| 50 |

**4** 33, 34, 35,

| 32 |
|----|
| 36 |
| 38 |

, 37

**5**

| 13 |
|----|
| 29 |
| 30 |

, 31, 32, 33, 34

## Lesson 5  Numbers 50 to 79

# Color.

51

69

Name: _____

# What comes before? Put a ✔.

 **1**

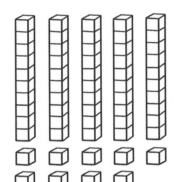 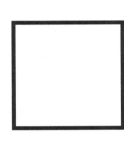 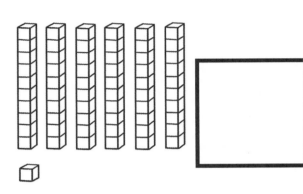

---

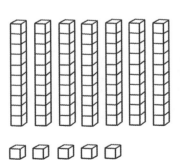 **2**

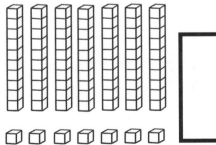 

# Which is the missing number? Color.

**1**

| 52 | 53 | 54 |  | 35 | 55 |

---

**2**

| 69 | 68 |  | 70 | 71 | 72 |

---

**3**

| 57 | 58 | 59 | 50 |  | 60 |

## Lesson 6  Numbers 80 to 100

# Color.

 **1**

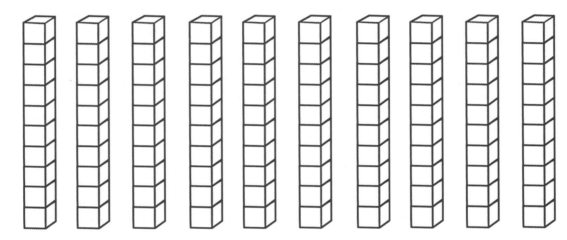

---

**2**

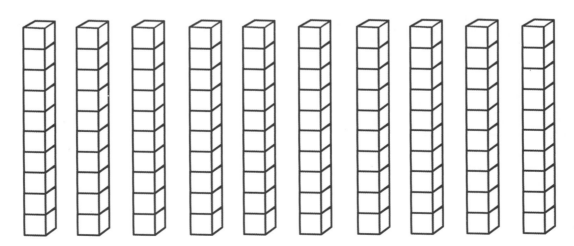

# What comes in between? Put a ✔.

 **1**

83 and 85

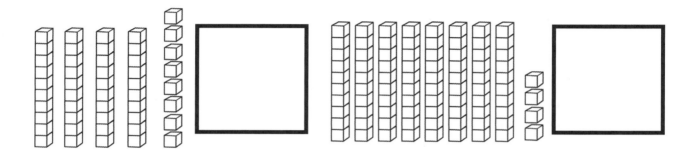

---

**2**

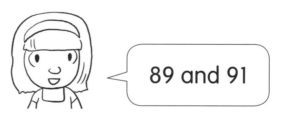

89 and 91

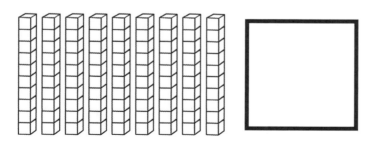

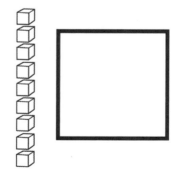

Name: _____

# What are the missing numbers from 88 to 92? Color.

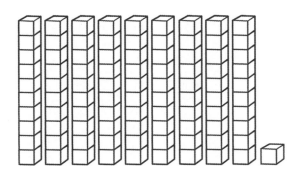

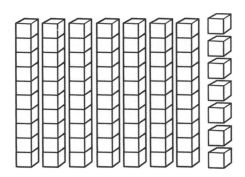

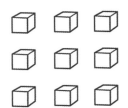

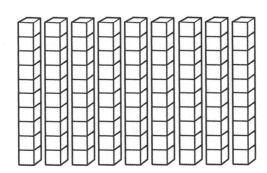

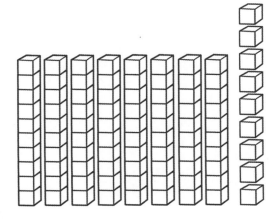

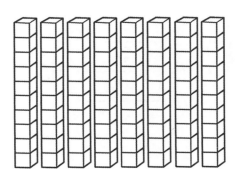

## Lesson 7  Numbers 1 to 100

# Use a 100 Chart. Color the missing number.

**1**  21, 31, | 32 | / 41 |, 51, 61

**2**  47, | 37 | / 57 |, 67, 77, 87

**3**  73, 74, 75, 76, | 77 | / 86 |

**4**  17, 18, 19, | 20 | / 29 |, 21

**5**  | 9 | / 20 |, 19, 29, 39, 49

**6**  35, | 36 | / 45 |, 55, 65, 75

Name: _____

# Use a 100 Chart. Put a ✔ if true.

  51 is after 50.

  89 is before 88.

  12 is after 22.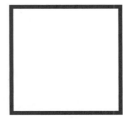

  70 is in between 69 and 61.

# CHAPTER 9 Comparing Sets

## Lesson 1  Comparing Sets of Up to 10

## Count and write.

**1** 

**2** 

**3** 

**4** 

**5** 

**6**

Name: _____

# Count, circle, and write.

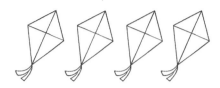

| 0 | 1 | 2 | 3 | 4 | 5 | 6 | 7 | 8 | 9 | 10 |

| 0 | 1 | 2 | 3 | 4 | 5 | 6 | 7 | 8 | 9 | 10 |

**3**

| 0 | 1 | 2 | 3 | 4 | 5 | 6 | 7 | 8 | 9 | 10 |

# Which has more? Color.
# Which has fewer? Circle.

 **1**

 **2**

**3**

### Lesson 2  Comparing Sets of 11 to 20

# Count and write.
# Circle the set with fewer.

# Match one-to-one.
# Then, color the set with more.

 **1**

**2**

**3**

**Name:** _____

## Lesson 3  Comparing Sets to Find the Difference

## Which has most? Color.
## Which has fewest? Circle.

  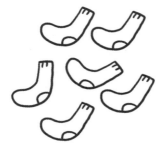

# Color the extra cubes blue.
# Count and write how many more.

 **1**

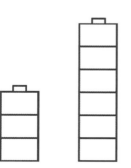 

 **2**

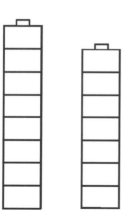 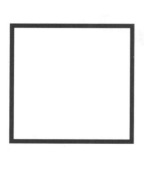

**3**

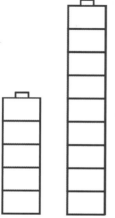 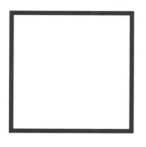

## Lesson 4 Combining Sets

## Count. Circle how many in all.

 **1**

 and

| 0 | 1 | 2 | 3 | 4 | 5 | 6 | 7 | 8 | 9 | 10 |
|---|---|---|---|---|---|---|---|---|---|----|

**2**

 and

| 0 | 1 | 2 | 3 | 4 | 5 | 6 | 7 | 8 | 9 | 10 |
|---|---|---|---|---|---|---|---|---|---|----|

**3**

 and

| 0 | 1 | 2 | 3 | 4 | 5 | 6 | 7 | 8 | 9 | 10 |
|---|---|---|---|---|---|---|---|---|---|----|

## Count and write.

 **1**

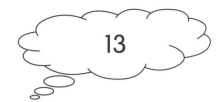

 and  is

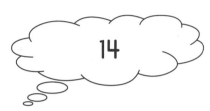

**2**

 and  is

**3**

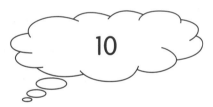

 and  is

# CHAPTER 10 Ordinal Numbers

**Lesson 1** **Sequencing Events**

## Color.

| first | next | last |
|:-----:|:----:|:----:|

| first | next | last |
|:-----:|:----:|:----:|

| first | next | last |
|:-----:|:----:|:----:|

## Color.

| first | second |
|-------|--------|
| third | last |

| first | second |
|-------|--------|
| third | last |

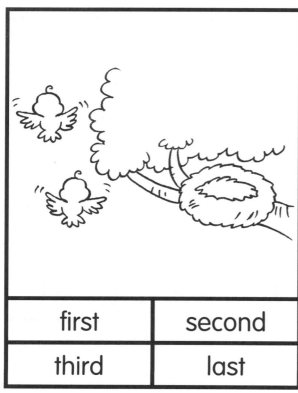

| first | second |
|-------|--------|
| third | last |

| first | second |
|-------|--------|
| third | last |

## Lesson 2 Physical Position

# Pair.

    •    •  1st

    •    •  2nd

    •    •  3rd

# Color the animal that comes before the lion.
# Circle the animal that comes after the lion.

**Lesson 3 Showing Your Preferences**

# Match. Then, compare with 2 friends.

3rd choice  •

2nd choice  •  •

1st choice  •  •

## Count and write.

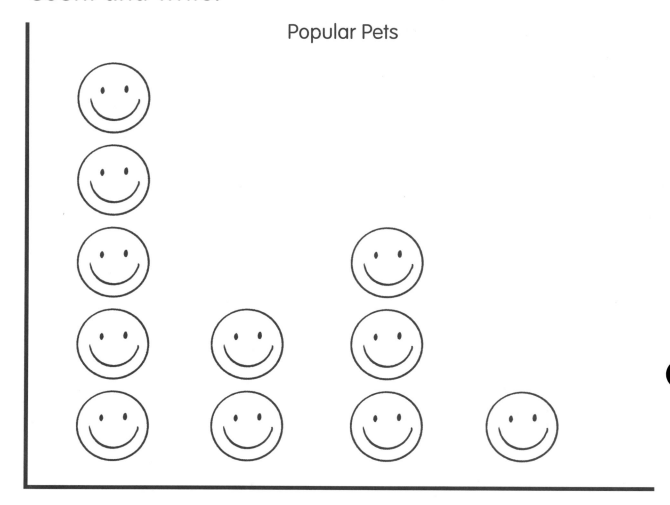

Popular Pets

Dog          Cat          Rabbit          Bird

1. How many like cats? _____

2. How many like rabbits? _____

3. How many like dogs? _____

4. How many like birds? _____

# CHAPTER 11 Calendar Patterns

## Lesson 1 Days of the Week

**Color a Saturday red. Say the date.**
**Color a Monday blue. Say the date.**
**Color a Thursday yellow. Say the date.**

| April 2011 | | | | | | |
|---|---|---|---|---|---|---|
| Monday | Tuesday | Wednesday | Thursday | Friday | Saturday | Sunday |
|  |  |  |  | 1 | 2 | 3 |
| 4 | 5 | 6 | 7 | 8 | 9 | 10 |
| 11 | 12 | 13 | 14 | 15 | 16 | 17 |
| 18 | 19 | 20 | 21 | 22 | 23 | 24 |
| 25 | 26 | 27 | 28 | 29 | 30 |  |

## Circle.

Which day is April 21?

Tuesday     Thursday

Which day is the first day of the month?

Friday     Saturday

## Circle.

 **1**

Which day comes after Monday?

Thursday          Sunday          Tuesday

---

 **2**

Which day comes before Thursday?

Wednesday          Friday          Saturday

---

**3**

Which day comes between Friday and Sunday?

Monday          Saturday          Thursday

**Name:** _____

### Lesson 2 Months of the Year

## Which month comes next? Color.

January, February

| March | May |
|---|---|

June, July

| September | August |
|---|---|

October, November

| December | September |
|---|---|

April, May

| July | June |
|---|---|

August, September

| November | October |
|---|---|

Make an X on the month <u>before</u> June.
Circle the month <u>after</u> January.
Color green the month <u>between</u> June and August.
Color yellow the months <u>between</u> August and
November.

| | | |
|---|---|---|
| January | February | March |
| April | May | June |
| July | August | September |
| October | November | December |

Name: _____

# CHAPTER 12 Counting On and Counting Back

Lesson 1  Counting On to 10

## Read and color.

**1** Which number comes after 7?

| 6 | 5 | 8 | 4 |

**2** Which number comes before 1?

| 10 | 0 | 2 | 11 |

**3** Which number comes after 4?

| 5 | 1 | 3 | 2 |

**4** Which number comes after 8?

| 7 | 0 | 1 | 9 |

# How many more to make 10? Count and write.

 **1**

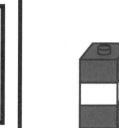 **2**

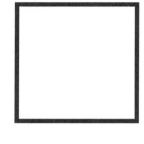

 **3**

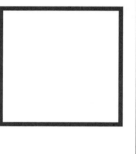

**4**

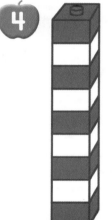

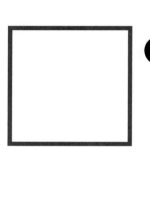

 **5**

 **6**

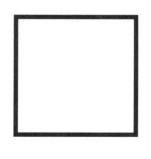

# How many more to make 10? Count and write.

 **1**

2 ☐

 **2**

5 ☐

 **3**

4 ☐

**4**

1 ☐

 **5**

3 ☐

**6**

6 ☐

## Lesson 2  Counting Back Using Fingers

# Look at the picture. Count and write.

1. How many boys are there in all?  _____

2. How many big boys are there in all?  _____

3. How many small boys are there in all? _____

4. How many bats are there in all?  _____

5. How many  are there in all?  _____

6. How many  are there in all?  _____

Name: _____

# Color, count, and write.

 **1**

There are 10  and  .

There is 1  so color 1 ◯.

◯ ◯ ◯ ◯ ◯ ◯ ◯ ◯ ◯ ◯

How many ◯ left? _____

How many  ? _____

 **2**

There are 10  and  .

There are 6  so color 6 ◯.

◯ ◯ ◯ ◯ ◯ ◯ ◯ ◯ ◯ ◯

How many ◯ left? _____

How many  ? _____

## Lesson 3  Finding Differences Using Fingers

# Which has more? Which has fewer?
# Color *more* or *fewer*.

| more | fewer |
|------|-------|

| more | fewer |
|------|-------|

| more | fewer |
|------|-------|

| more | fewer |
|------|-------|

**Name:** _____

## Look at the picture. Count.

## Color.

Are there more  or  ?

Are there fewer  or  ?

## Write.

How many more  are there? _____

How many fewer  are there? _____

# CHAPTER 13 Patterns

## Lesson 1 Repeating Patterns

The shapes follow a repeating pattern.
Draw the missing shapes to complete the pattern.

**1**

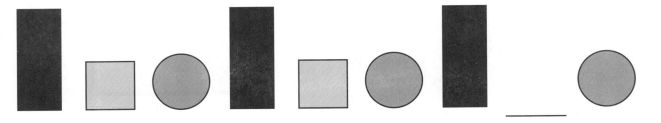

**2**

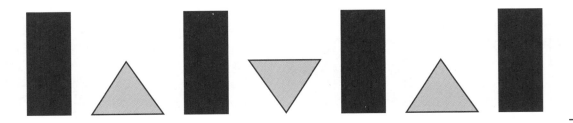

**3**

**Extra Practice KB**

Name: _____

# The objects follow a repeating pattern.
# Circle the object that comes next.

 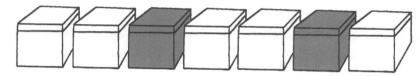  

# Tell about the pattern.
# What is the pattern unit? Draw.

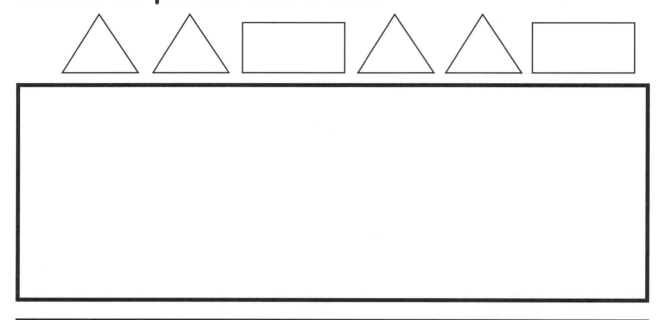

# Number Facts

**Lesson 1  Number Facts to 10**

## Count and write.

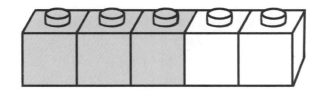

There are _____ .

There are _____ .

5 is _____ and _____ .

---

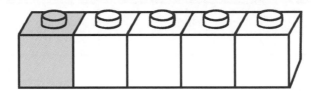

There is _____ .

There are _____ .

5 is _____ and _____ .

## Count and write.

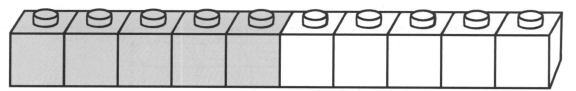

There are _____  .

There are _____ ⬜ .

10 is _____ and _____ .

---

**2**

There are _____ ⬜ .

There are _____ ⬜ .

10 is _____ and _____ .

# Count and write.

**1**    10 is _____ and 7.

**2**    4 and 5 are _____ .

**3**    7 is 2 and _____ .

**4**    _____ and 6 are 9.

**5**    _____ and 2 are 5.

**6**    8 is _____ and 0.

**7**    6 and _____ are 7.

# Count and draw more .

 **1**

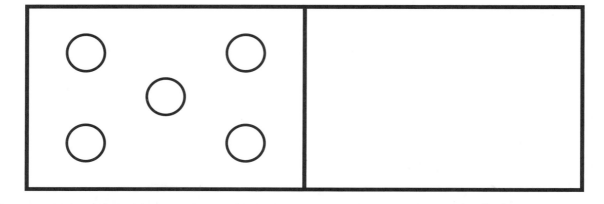

**2**

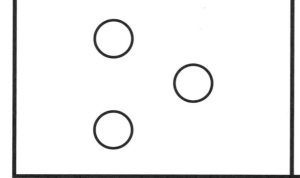

## Lesson 2  Combining Sets

# Count and write.

Count how many. _____

 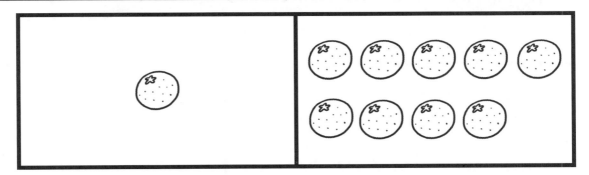

Count how many. _____

 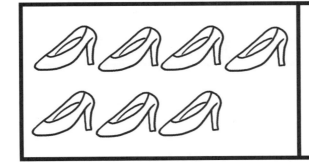 

Count how many. _____

## Count and write.

 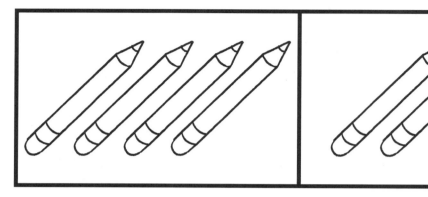

Count how many. _____

How many more to make 10? _____

 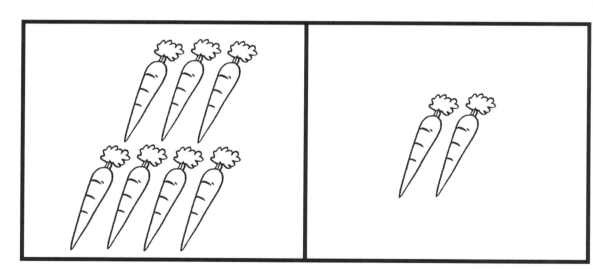

Count how many. _____

How many more to make 10? _____

## Lesson 3  Composing and Decomposing Numbers to 20

## Draw ◯. Write the number sentence.

6

_____ is _____ and _____ .

2

18

_____ is _____ and _____ .

# Count and write. Write the number sentence.

_____ and _____ make _____ .

_____ and _____ make _____ .

 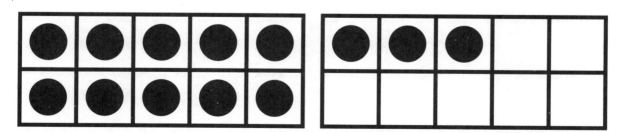

_____ and _____ make _____ .

**Name:** _____

## Lesson 4  Counting On

## Count and write.

Count how many.                                      _____

How many more to make 15?                _____

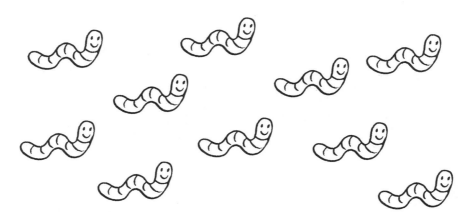

Count how many.                                      _____

How many more to make 15?                _____

Name: _____

# Count and write.

Count how many. _____

How many more to make 15? _____

Count how many. _____

How many more to make 15? _____

**Extra Practice KB**

# CHAPTER  **15** Length and Height

## Lesson 1   Comparing Lengths

### Draw a **long** tail.

---

### Draw a **short** tail.

---

### Draw a **short** tail.

**1** **Color the balloon with the longest string red.**
**Color the balloon with the shortest string blue.**

 **2** **Color the longest train yellow.**
**Color the shortest train green.**

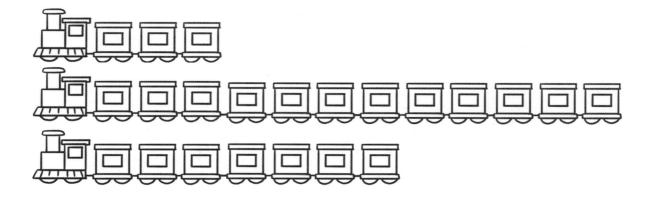

**Name:** _____

● **Read and color.**

toothbrush

pencil

eraser

① The pencil is the | shortest |
   | longest | .

② The eraser is the | shortest |
   | longest | .

③ The toothbrush is | shorter |
   | longer | than the eraser.

④ The pencil is | shorter |
   | longer | than the toothbrush.

**Name:** _____

### Lesson 2  Comparing Lengths Using Nonstandard Units

## Use connecting cubes.
## Measure, count, and write.

 **1**

The stick is about _____  long.

 **2**

The fork is about _____ long.

 **3**

The piece of chalk is about _____ long.

Name: _____

● **Count and write.**

The toothbrush is about _____ ⬭ long.

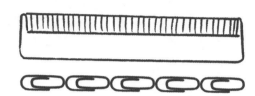

● The comb is about _____ ⬭ long.

The key is about _____ ⬭ long.

The toothbrush is about _____ ⬭ longer than the comb.

● The key is about _____ ⬭ shorter than the comb.

## Lesson 3  Comparing Heights Using Nonstandard Units

**1** The teddy bear is the

| shortest |
|----------|
| tallest |

.

**2** The doll is the

| shortest |
|----------|
| tallest |

.

**3** The robot is

| shorter |
|---------|
| taller |

than the doll.

**4** The robot is

| shorter |
|---------|
| taller |

than the teddy bear.

Name: _____

**Count and write.**
**Circle the shorter object.**

Picture A

Picture B

Picture A is about _____ high.

Picture B is about _____ high.

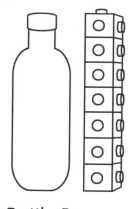
Bottle A          Bottle B

Bottle A is about _____ high.

Bottle B is about _____ high.

Name: _____

# Classifying and Sorting

## Lesson 1  Classifying Things by One Attribute

## Make an X on the object that does not belong.

 **1**

**2**

 **3**

Name: _____

## What is the same? Color.

 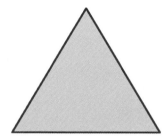

| color | shape | size |

---

| color | pattern | size |

---

  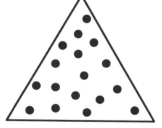

| color | shape | pattern |

## Lesson 2  Classifying and Sorting Things by Two Attributes

**Color the big squares red.**
**Color the big rectangles yellow.**
**Color the small triangles blue.**
**Make an *X* on the small circles.**

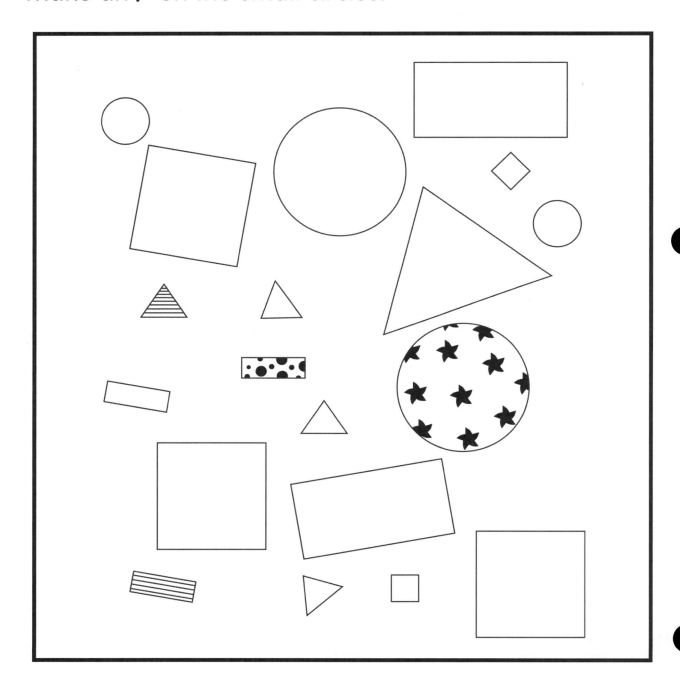

Name: _____

## Color these red.
## Draw 2 more circles.

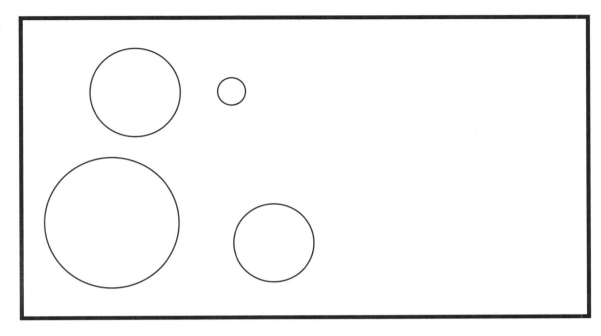

## Color these green.
## Draw 3 more rectangles.

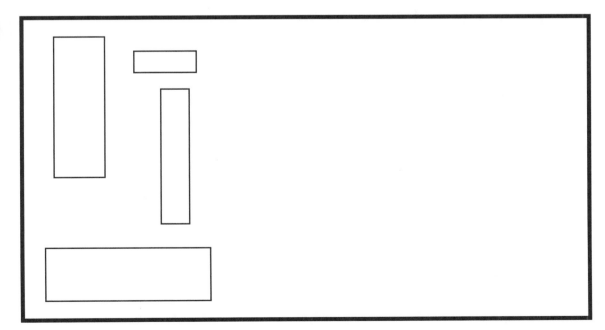

# Match.

  •                    •  **triangle**

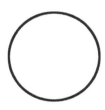  •                    •  **circle**

  •                    •  **big**

  •                    •  **small**

# CHAPTER 17 Addition Stories

Lesson 1 **Writing Addition Sentences and Representing Addition Stories**

## Count and write.

 **1**

 plus  is equal to

[ ] ⊕ [ ] ⊜ [ ]

---

**2**

 plus  is equal to

[ ] ○ [ ] ○ [ ]

---

**3**

 plus  is equal to

[ ] ○ [ ] ○ [ ]

# Count and write.

 **1**  plus  is equal to

 **2** plus  is equal to

 **3**  plus  is equal to

# Count and write.

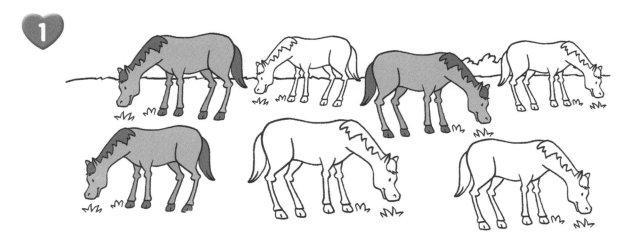

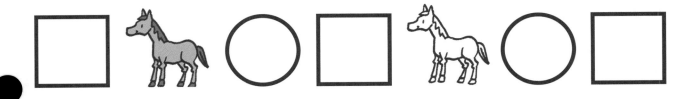

---

## Lesson 2  Addition Facts to 5

### Write.

**1**  $1 + 3 =$ _____ .

**2**  $2 + 3 =$ _____ .

**3**  $5 + 0 =$ _____ .

**4**  $1 + 2 =$ _____ .

**5**  $4 + 1 =$ _____ .

**6**  $3 + 0 =$ _____ .

**7**  $0 + 4 =$ _____ .

Name: _____

# Write.

1. $2 + 2 =$ _____ .

2. $1 + 4 =$ _____ .

3. $1 + 0 =$ _____ .

4. $3 + 2 =$ _____ .

5. $1 + 1 =$ _____ .

6. $0 + 2 =$ _____ .

7. $0 + 5 =$ _____ .

 **CHAPTER 18** **Subtraction Stories**

**Lesson 1** Writing Subtraction Sentences and Representing Subtraction Stories

## Count and write.

  minus  is equal to

  minus  is equal to

 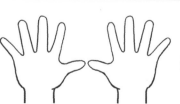 minus  is equal to

© 2012 Marshall Cavendish International (Singapore) Private Limited. Copying is permitted; see page ii.

**Extra Practice KB**

Name: _____

# Count and write.

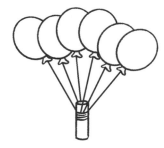 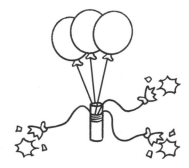 

| There are 6 balloons. | 3 balloons burst. | How many are left? |

---

| There are 7 birds. | 5 birds fly away. | How many are left? |

© 2012 Marshall Cavendish International (Singapore) Private Limited. Copying is permitted; see page ii.

**Extra Practice KB**   **85**

# Count and write. Then, tell a story.

**1**

---

**2**

Lesson 2  Comparing Sets

## How many more? Write the number sentence.

How many more  ?

___

There are ☐ more 🍴.

# How many more? Write the number sentence.

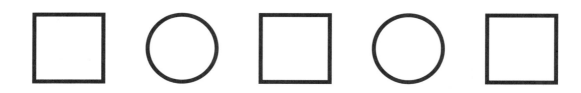

There are _____ more .

---

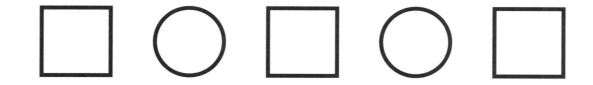

There are _____ more .

## Lesson 3  Subtraction Facts to 5

# Count and write.

**1** ❤  3 − 1 = _____ .

**2** ✿  3 − 2 = _____ .

**3** 🎈  5 − 0 = _____ .

**4** 🍎  2 − 1 = _____ .

**5** ☁  4 − 2 = _____ .

**6** 🍃  3 − 3 = _____ .

**7** 🧢  4 − 1 = _____ .

# Write the number sentence.

 **1**

---

**2**

---

**3**

Name: _____

# Measurement

## Lesson 1  Comparing Weights Using Nonstandard Units

**Circle the lighter object.**
**Color the heavier object.**

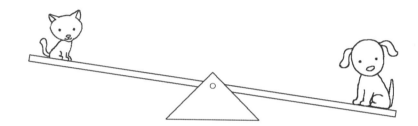

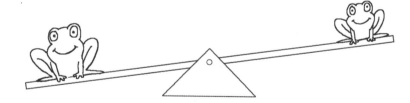

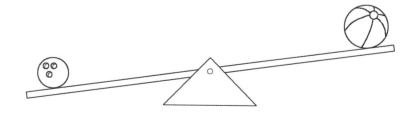

# Count and write.

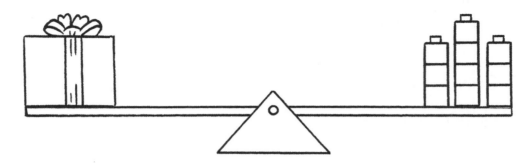

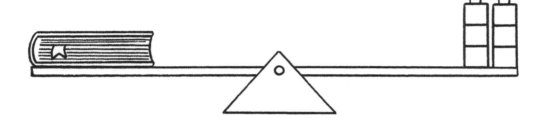

The box weighs about  .

The book weighs about .

# Circle the heavier object.

Name: _____

## Lesson 2  Comparing Capacities

**Circle the container that holds more.**

**Make an X on the container that holds less.**

**Color the containers that hold the same amount.**

# Count and write. Then, color.

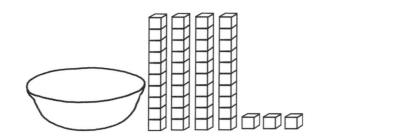

The  holds about _____ ▢.

The  holds about _____ ▢.

The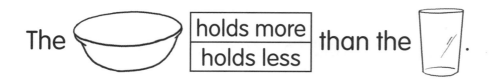

The [bowl] | holds more / holds less | than the [glass].

The [glass] | holds more / holds less | than the [bowl].

**Extra Practice KB**

Name: _____

## Lesson 3  Comparing Events in Time
# Which takes more time? Circle.

---

# Which takes less time? Circle.

## Copy the pictures. Then, color the picture you took more time to draw.

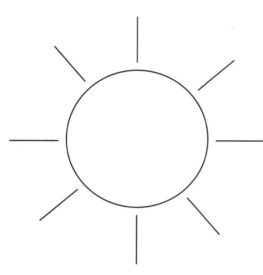

Name: _____

# CHAPTER 20 Money

### Lesson 1  Coin Values

## Color the correct value red.

| 25¢ | 5¢ | 1¢ | 10¢ |
|---|---|---|---|

| 1¢ | 10¢ | 25¢ | 5¢ |
|---|---|---|---|

| 10¢ | 25¢ | 5¢ | 1¢ |
|---|---|---|---|

| 5¢ | 1¢ | 10¢ | 25¢ |
|---|---|---|---|

# How were the coins sorted? Read and color.

I have groups of silver coins and bronze coins.

| color | size | value |

---

I have groups of pennies, nickels, dimes, and quarters.

| color | size | value |

---

I have groups of big coins and small coins.

| color | size | value |

## Lesson 2 Counting Coins

# How many pennies do you need? Color them brown.

 and

5¢ and 2¢

 and  and

3¢ and 3¢ and 4¢

# How much is needed? Circle the purse.

 **1**

14¢

---

**2**

20¢

---

**3**

and

6¢    3¢

# Chapter 7 Answers

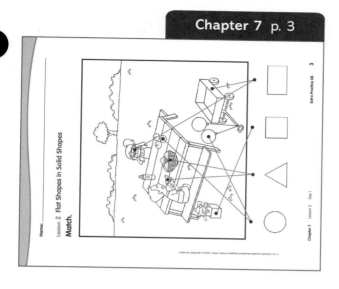

Name:

Lesson 2 Flat Shapes in Solid Shapes

**Match.**

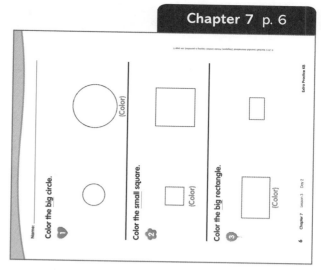

Name:

1 Color the big circle.

2 Color the small square.

3 Color the big rectangle.

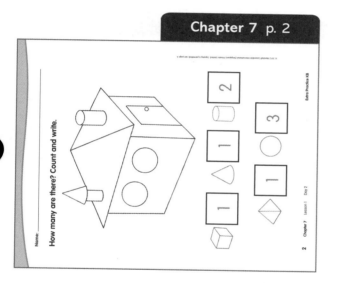

Name:

**How many are there? Count and write.**

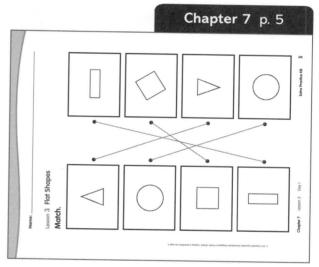

Name:

Lesson 3 Flat Shapes

**Match.**

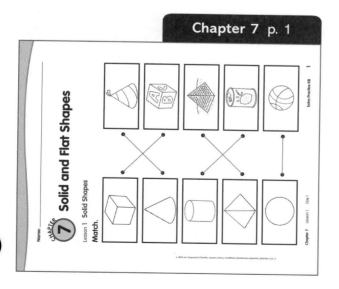

Name:

**CHAPTER 7 Solid and Flat Shapes**

Lesson 1 Solid Shapes

**Match.**

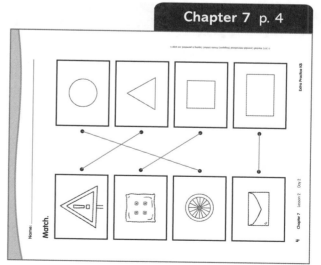

Name:

**Match.**

# Chapter 7 Answers

## Chapter 7 p. 8

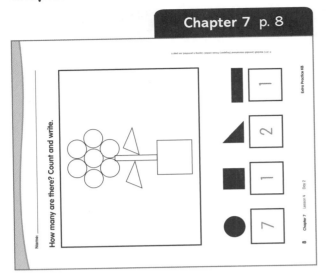

## Chapter 7 p. 10

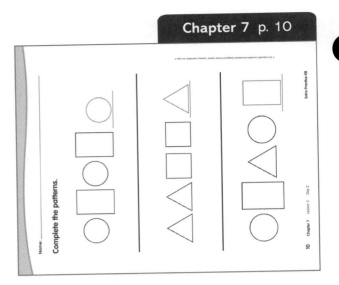

## Chapter 7 p. 7

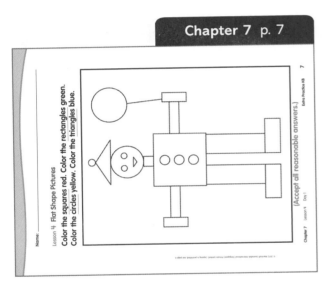

## Chapter 7 p. 9

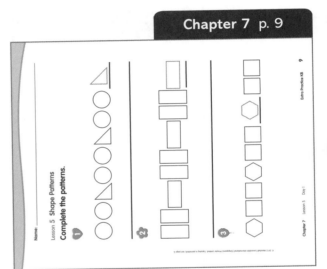

# Chapter 8 Answers

## Chapter 8 p. 11

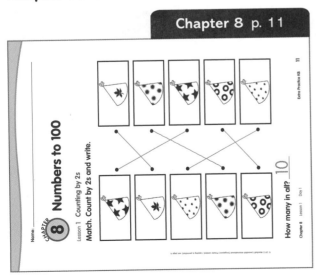

## Chapter 8 p. 12

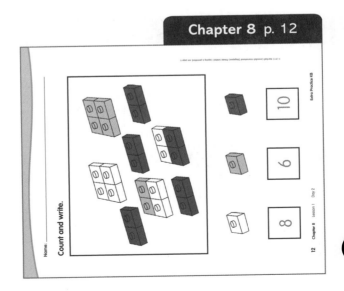

# Chapter 8 Answers

## Chapter 8 p. 15

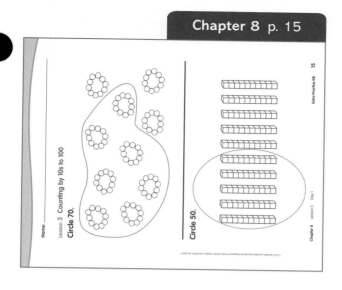

## Chapter 8 p. 18

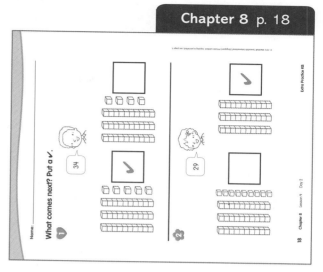

## Chapter 8 p. 14

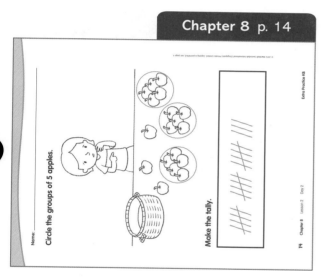

## Chapter 8 p. 17

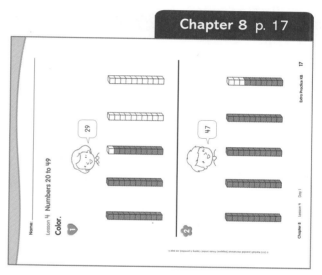

## Chapter 8 p. 13

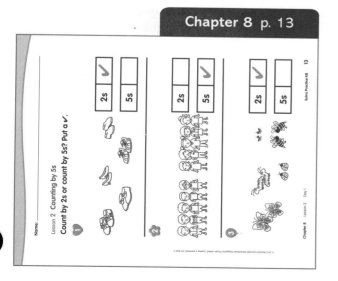

## Chapter 8 p. 16

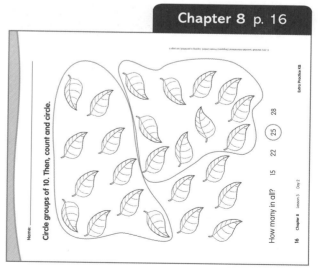

# Chapter 8 Answers

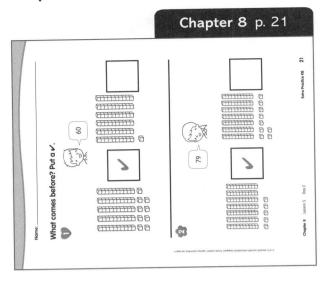

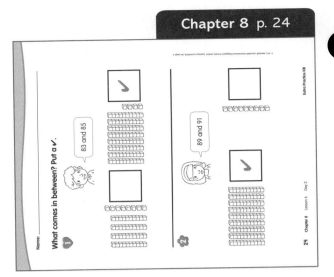

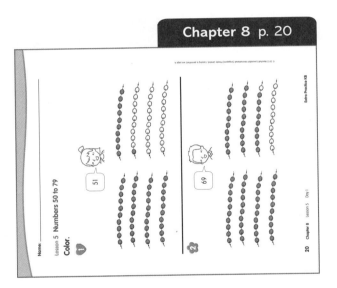

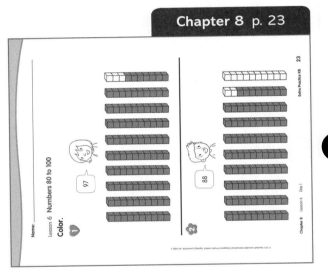

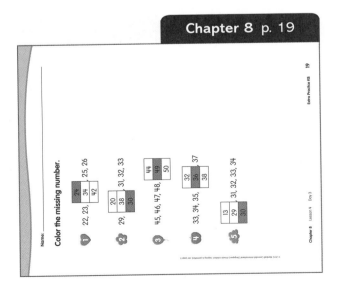

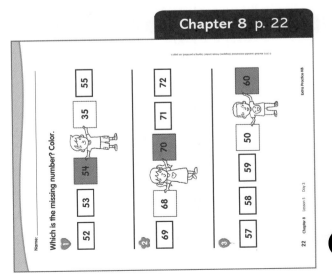

# Chapter 8 Answers

## Chapter 8 p. 26

Name:

Lesson 7 Numbers 1 to 100

**Use a 100 Chart. Color the missing number.**

1. 21, 31, | 32 / 41 | 51, 61
2. 47, | 37 / 57 | 67, 77, 87
3. 73, 74, 75, 76, | 77 / 86 |
4. 17, 18, 19, | 20 / 29 | 21
5. | 9 / 20 | 19, 29, 39, 49
6. 35, | 36 / 45 | 55, 65, 75

26   Chapter 8   Lesson 7   Day 1

Extra Practice KB

## Chapter 8 p. 25

Name:

**What are the missing numbers from 88 to 92?**
**Color.**

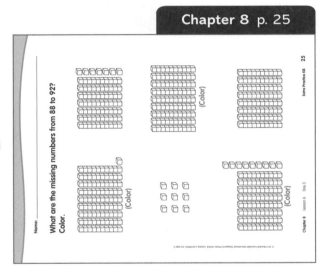

(Color)

(Color)

(Color)

Chapter 8   Lesson 6   Day 3

Extra Practice KB   25

## Chapter 8 p. 27

Name:

**Use a 100 Chart. Put a ✔ if true.**

1. 51 is after 50. ✔
2. 89 is before 88.
3. 12 is after 22.
4. 70 is in between 69 and 61.

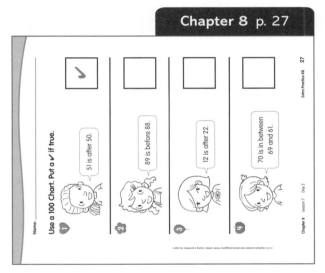

Chapter 8   Lesson 7   Day 2

Extra Practice KB   27

# Chapter 9 Answers

## Chapter 9 p. 28

Name:

### 9 Comparing Sets

Lesson 1  Comparing Sets of Up to 10

**Count and write.**

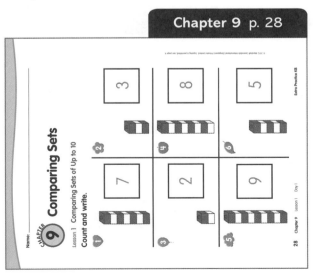

1. 7
2. 3
3. 2
4. 8
5. 9
6. 5

28   Chapter 9   Lesson 1   Day 1

Extra Practice KB

## Chapter 9 p. 29

Name:

**Count, circle, and write.**

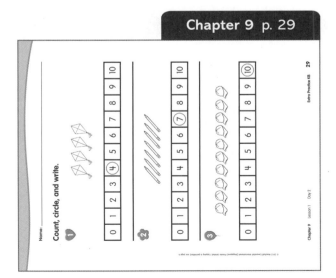

1. 0 1 2 3 (4) 5 6 7 8 9 10
2. 0 1 2 3 4 5 6 (7) 8 9 10
3. 0 1 2 3 4 5 6 7 8 9 (10)

Chapter 9   Lesson 1   Day 2

Extra Practice KB   29

# Chapter 9 Answers

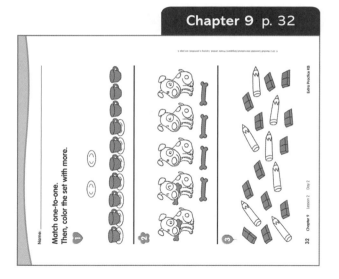

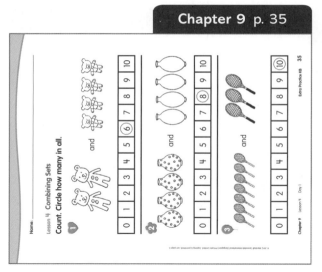

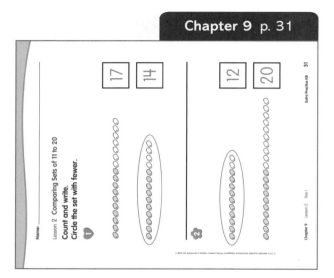

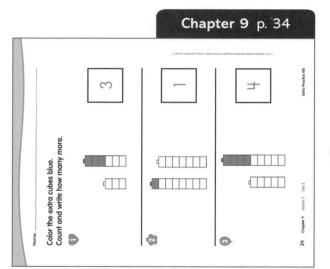

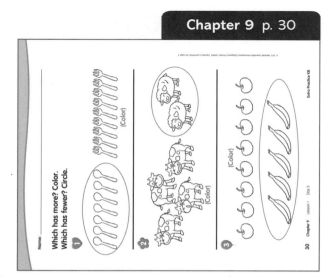

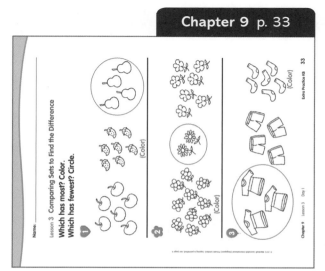

## Chapter 9 Answers

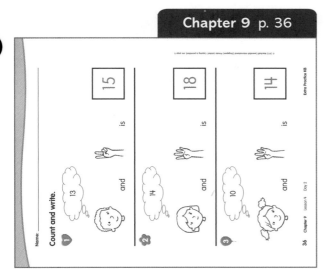

## Chapter 10 Answers

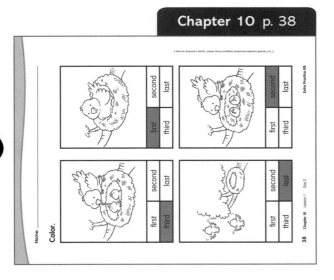

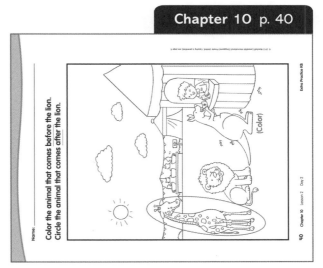

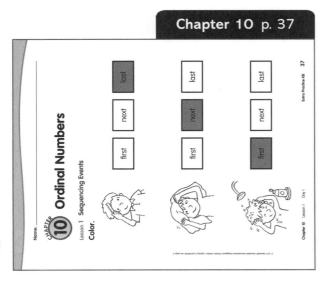

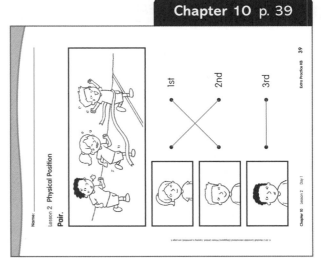

# Chapter 10 Answers

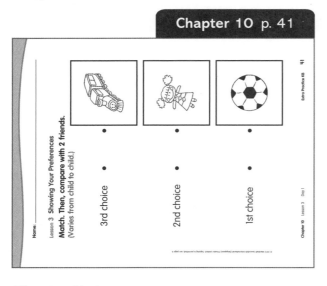

Name: _____

Lesson 3  Showing Your Preferences

Match. Then, compare with 2 friends.
(Varies from child to child.)

3rd choice

2nd choice

1st choice

Chapter 10  Lesson 3  Day 1

Extra Practice KB  41

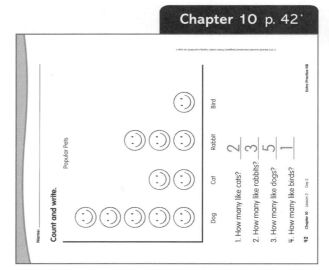

Name: _____

Count and write.

Popular Pets

Dog    Cat    Rabbit    Bird

1. How many like cats?  2
2. How many like rabbits?  3
3. How many like dogs?  5
4. How many like birds?  1

42  Chapter 10  Lesson 3  Day 2

Extra Practice KB

# Chapter 11  Answers

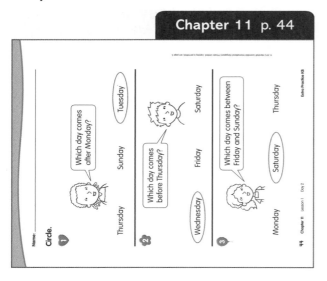

Name: _____

Circle.

1  Which day comes after Monday?

Thursday    Sunday    Tuesday

2  Which day comes before Thursday?

Wednesday    Friday    Saturday

3  Which day comes between Friday and Sunday?

Monday    Saturday    Thursday

44  Chapter 11  Lesson 1  Day 2

Extra Practice KB

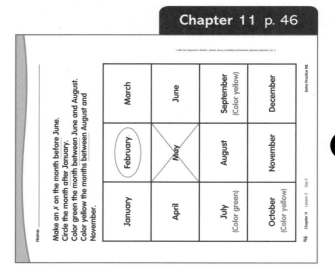

Name: _____

Make an X on the month before June.
Circle the month after January.
Color green the month between June and August.
Color yellow the months between August and November.

| January | February | March |
|---|---|---|
| April | May | June |
| July (Color green) | August | September (Color yellow) |
| October (Color yellow) | November | December |

46  Chapter 11  Lesson 2  Day 2

Extra Practice KB

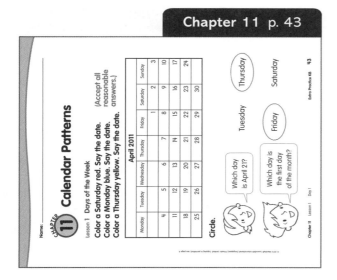

Name: _____

## CHAPTER 11 Calendar Patterns

Lesson 1  Days of the Week

Color a Saturday red. Say the date.
Color a Monday blue. Say the date.
Color a Thursday yellow. Say the date.

(Accept all reasonable answers.)

April 2011

| Monday | Tuesday | Wednesday | Thursday | Friday | Saturday | Sunday |
|---|---|---|---|---|---|---|
| | | | | 1 | 2 | 3 |
| 4 | 5 | 6 | 7 | 8 | 9 | 10 |
| 11 | 12 | 13 | 14 | 15 | 16 | 17 |
| 18 | 19 | 20 | 21 | 22 | 23 | 24 |
| 25 | 26 | 27 | 28 | 29 | 30 | |

Circle.

Which day is April 21?    Tuesday    Thursday

Which day is the first day of the month?    Friday    Saturday

Chapter 11  Lesson 1  Day 1

Extra Practice KB  43

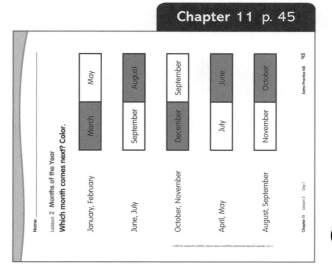

Name: _____

Lesson 2  Months of the Year

Which month comes next? Color.

January, February    March    May

June, July    September    August

October, November    December    September

April, May    July    June

August, September    November    October

Chapter 11  Lesson 2  Day 1

Extra Practice KB  45

# Chapter 12 Answers

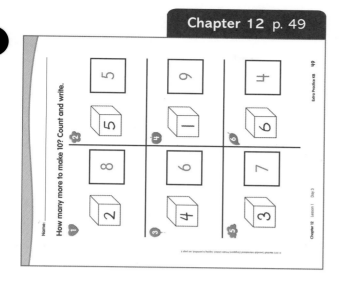

**Chapter 12 p. 49**

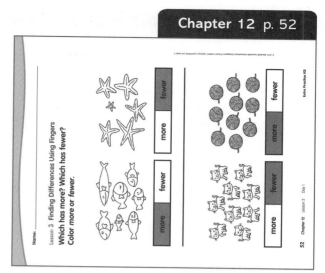

**Chapter 12 p. 52**

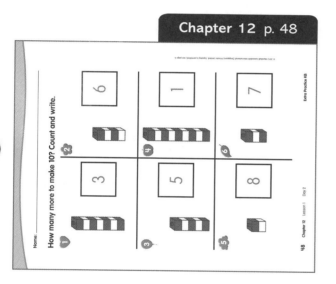

**Chapter 12 p. 48**

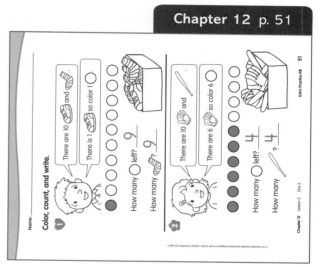

**Chapter 12 p. 51**

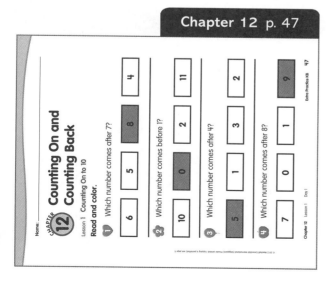

**Chapter 12 p. 47**

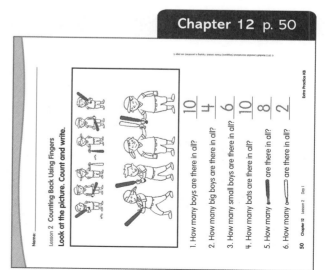

**Chapter 12 p. 50**

# Chapter 12 Answers

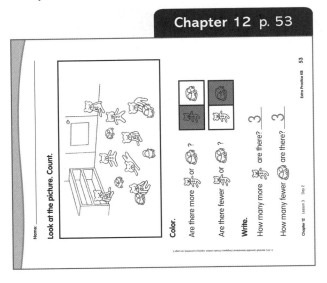

# Chapter 13 Answers

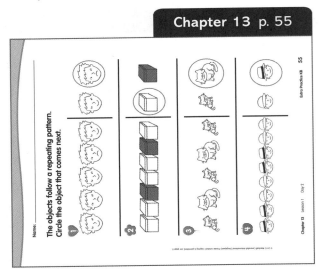

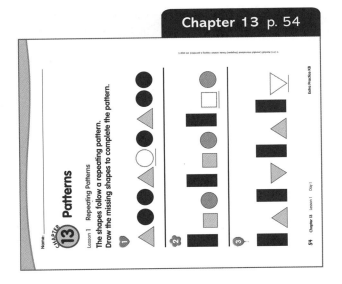

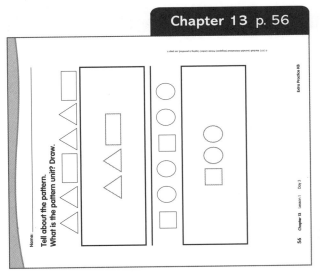

# Chapter 14 Answers

## Chapter 14 p. 59

Name: _____

**Count and write.**

1. 10 is __3__ and 7.

2. 4 and 5 are __9__.

3. 7 is 2 and __5__.

4. __3__ and 6 are 9.

5. __3__ and 2 are 5.

6. 8 is __8__ and 0.

7. 6 and __1__ are 7.

Chapter 14   Lesson 1   Day 3

Extra Practice KB   59

## Chapter 14 p. 62

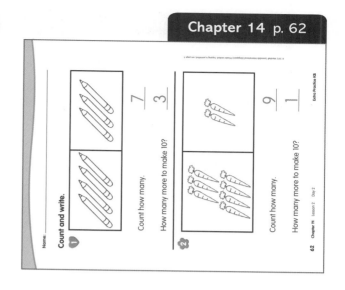

Name: _____

**Count and write.**

1. Count how many. __7__
   How many more to make 10? __3__

2. Count how many. __9__
   How many more to make 10? __1__

Chapter 14   Lesson 2   Day 2

Extra Practice KB   62

## Chapter 14 p. 58

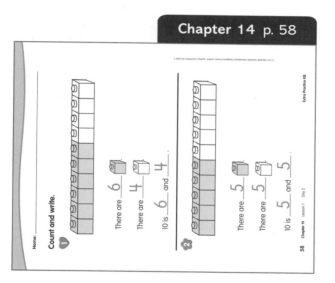

Name: _____

**Count and write.**

1. There are __6__
   There are __4__
   10 is __6__ and __4__.

2. There are __5__
   There are __5__
   10 is __5__ and __5__.

Chapter 14   Lesson 1   Day 2

Extra Practice KB   58

## Chapter 14 p. 61

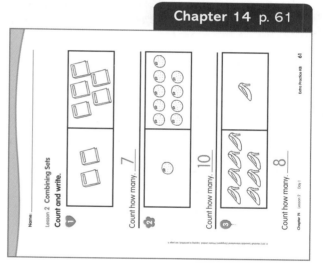

Name: _____

**Lesson 2  Combining Sets**
**Count and write.**

1. Count how many. __7__

2. Count how many. __10__

3. Count how many. __8__

Chapter 14   Lesson 2   Day 1

Extra Practice KB   61

## Chapter 14 p. 57

Name: _____

**14 Number Facts**

Lesson 1  Number Facts to 10
**Count and write.**

1. There are __3__
   There are __2__
   5 is __3__ and __2__.

2. There is __1__
   There are __4__
   5 is __1__ and __4__.

Chapter 14   Lesson 1   Day 1

Extra Practice KB   57

## Chapter 14 p. 60

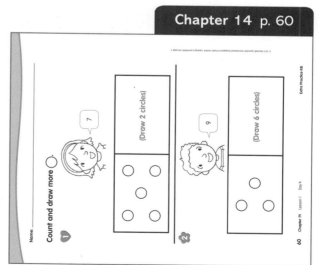

Name: _____

**Count and draw more ◯.**

1. 7
   (Draw 2 circles)

2. 9
   (Draw 6 circles)

Chapter 14   Lesson 1   Day 4

Extra Practice KB   60

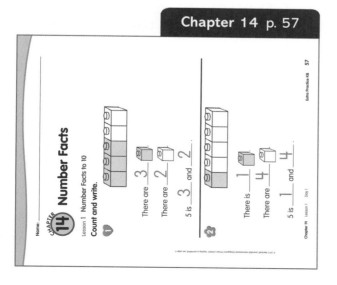

# Chapter 14 Answers

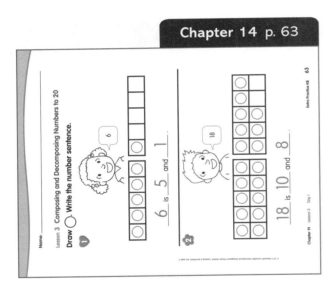

Name: _____

**Count and write. Write the number sentence.**

1
5 and 4 make 9 .

2
4 and 0 make 4 .

3
10 and 3 make 13 .

Chapter 14　Lesson 3　Day 2　　64　Extra Practice KB

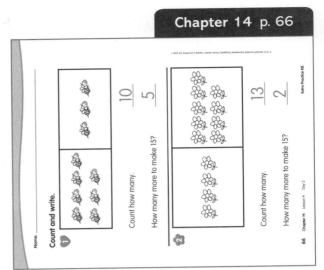

Name: _____

**Count and write.**

1
Count how many. 10

How many more to make 15? 5

2
Count how many. 13

How many more to make 15? 2

Chapter 14　Lesson 4　Day 2　　66　Extra Practice KB

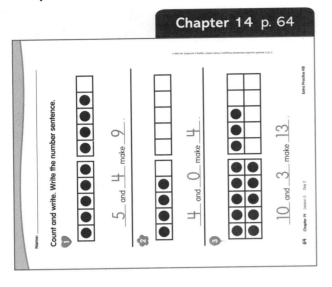

Name: _____

Lesson 3  Composing and Decomposing Numbers to 20
**Draw ◯. Write the number sentence.**

1
6
6 is 5 and 1 .

2
18
18 is 10 and 8 .

Chapter 14　Lesson 3　Day 1　　63　Extra Practice KB

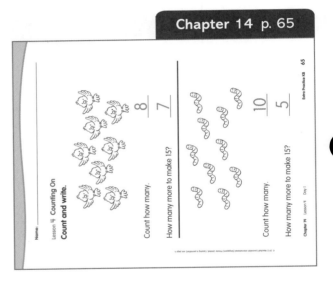

Name: _____

Lesson 4  Counting On
**Count and write.**

Count how many. 8

How many more to make 15? 7

Count how many. 10

How many more to make 15? 5

Chapter 14　Lesson 4　Day 1　　65　Extra Practice KB

# Chapter 15  Answers

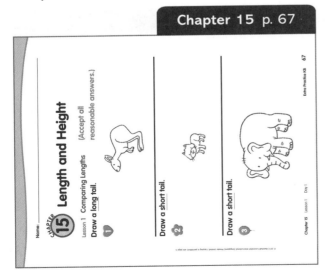

Name: _____

## 15 Length and Height

(Accept all reasonable answers.)

Lesson 1  Comparing Lengths
**Draw a long tail.**

1

2 Draw a short tail.

3 Draw a short tail.

Chapter 15　Lesson 1　Day 1　　67　Extra Practice KB

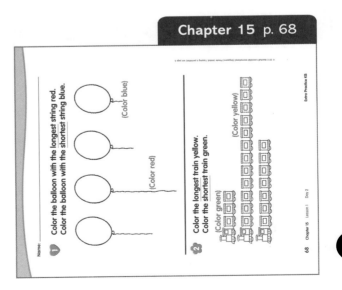

Name: _____

1
**Color the balloon with the longest string red.**
**Color the balloon with the shortest string blue.**

(Color red)　　(Color blue)

2
**Color the longest train yellow.**
**Color the shortest train green.**

(Color green)　　(Color yellow)

Chapter 15　Lesson 1　Day 2　　68　Extra Practice KB

# Chapter 15 Answers

## Chapter 15 p. 71

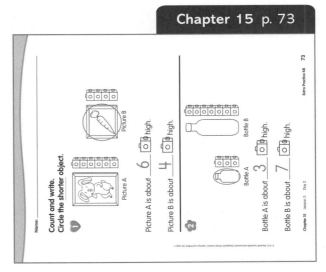

Name:

**Count and write.**

The toothbrush is about __8__ 🔗 long.

The comb is about __5__ 🔗 long.

The key is about __3__ 🔗 long.

The toothbrush is about __3__ 🔗 longer than the comb.

The key is about __2__ 🔗 shorter than the comb.

Chapter 15   Lesson 2   Day 2

Extra Practice KB   **71**

## Chapter 15 p. 70

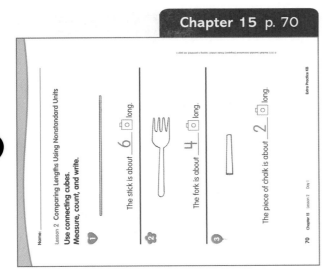

Name:

Lesson 2  Comparing Lengths Using Nonstandard Units
**Use connecting cubes.**
**Measure, count, and write.**

1. The stick is about __6__ 🔲 long.

2. The fork is about __4__ 🔲 long.

3. The piece of chalk is about __2__ 🔲 long.

**70**   Chapter 15   Lesson 2   Day 1

Extra Practice KB

## Chapter 15 p. 73

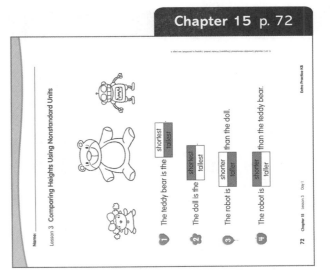

Name:

**Count and write.**
**Circle the shorter object.**

1. Picture A is about __6__ 🔲 high.

   Picture B is about __4__ 🔲 high.

2. Bottle A is about __3__ 🔲 high.

   Bottle B is about __7__ 🔲 high.

Chapter 15   Lesson 3   Day 2

Extra Practice KB   **73**

## Chapter 15 p. 69

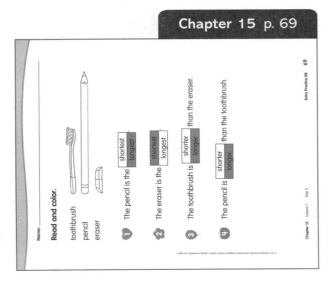

Name:

**Read and color.**

toothbrush
pencil
eraser

1. The pencil is the [shortest | **longest**]

2. The eraser is the [shortest | **longest**]

3. The toothbrush is [**shorter** | longer] than the eraser.

4. The pencil is [**shorter** | longer] than the toothbrush.

Chapter 15   Lesson 1   Day 3

Extra Practice KB   **69**

## Chapter 15 p. 72

Name:

Lesson 3  Comparing Heights Using Nonstandard Units

1. The teddy bear is the [shortest | **tallest**]

2. The doll is the [**shortest** | tallest]

3. The robot is [shorter | **taller**] than the doll.

4. The robot is [**shorter** | taller] than the teddy bear.

**72**   Chapter 15   Lesson 3   Day 1

Extra Practice KB

Extra Practice KB   **113**

# Chapter 16 Answers

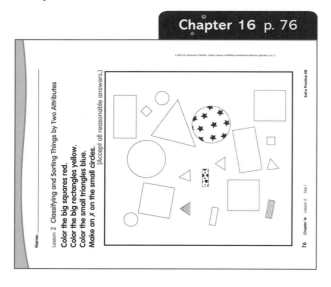

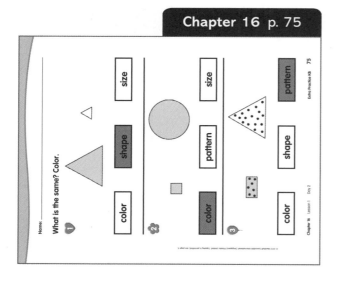

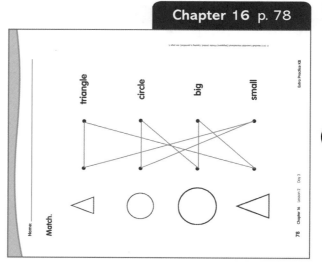

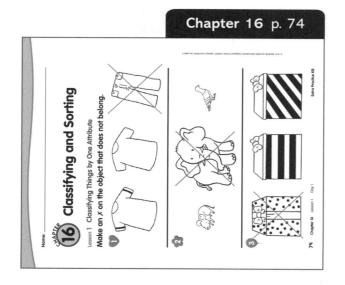

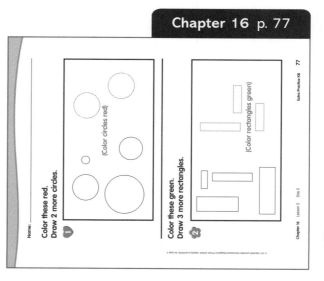

# Chapter 17 Answers

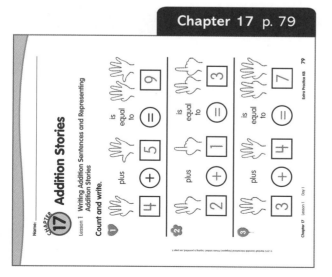

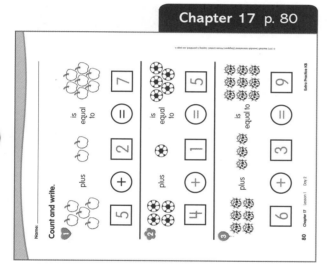

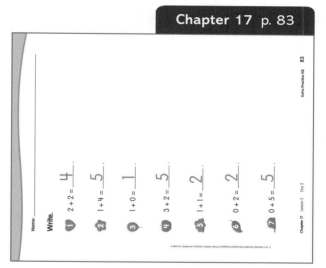

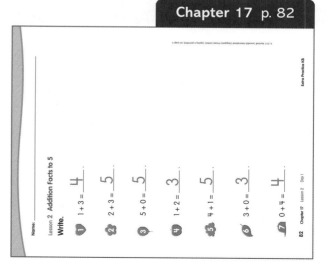

# Chapter 18 Answers

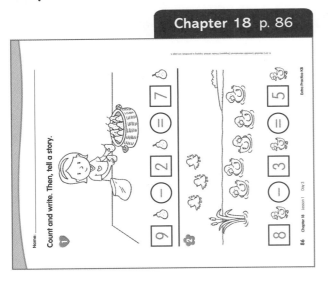

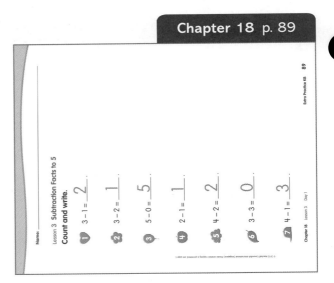

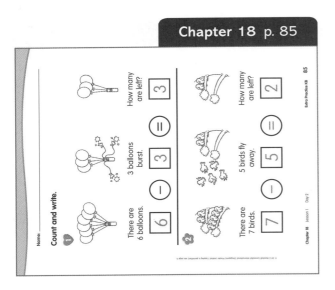

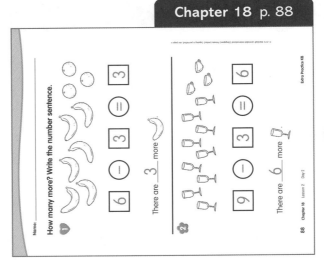

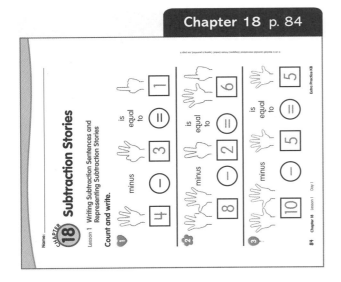

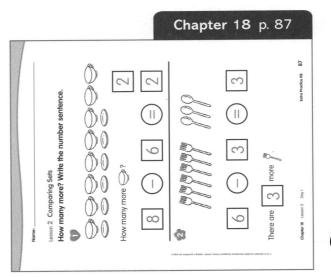

## Chapter 18 Answers

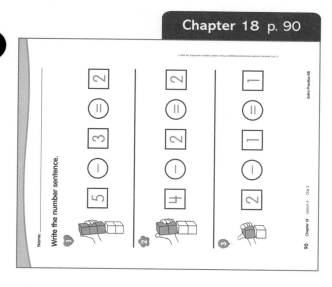

## Chapter 19 Answers

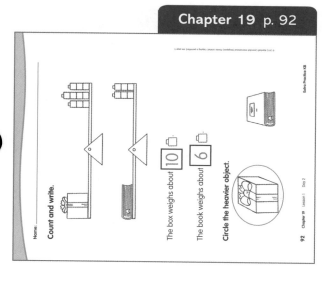

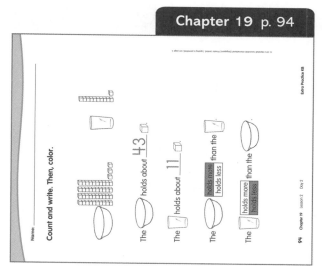

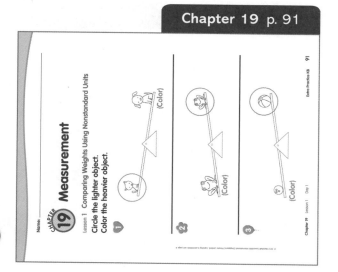

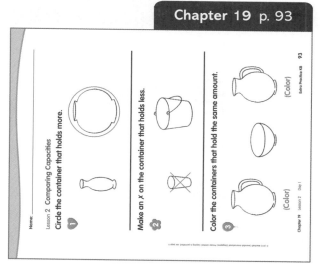

# Chapter 19 Answers

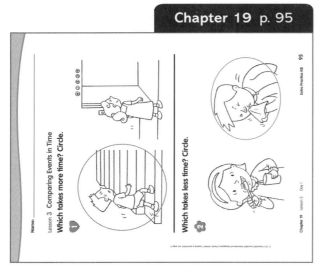

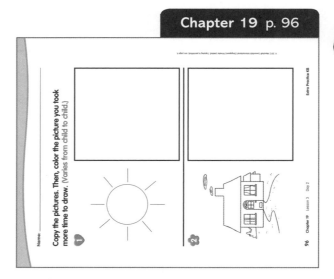

# Chapter 20 Answers

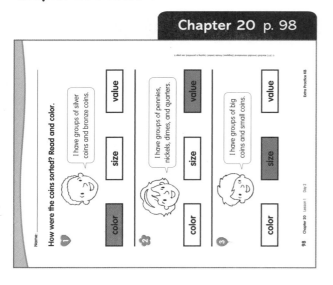

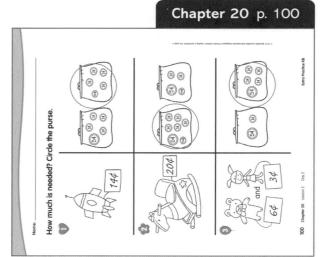

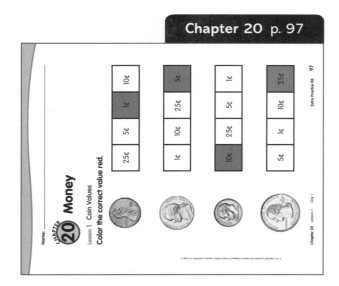

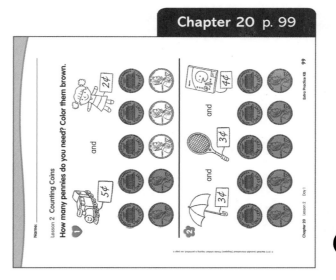